THE BEST OF

NAT KING COLE

Contents

Edited by Peter Foss

First Published 1989
© International Music Publications

Exclusive Distributors
International Music Publications
Southend Road, Woodford Green,
Essex IG8 8HN, England

ANSWER ME

English Lyric by CARL SIGMAN
Music by GERHARD WINKLER and FRED RAUCH

A BLOSSOM FELL

Words and Music by HOWARD BARNES,
HAROLD CORNELIUS and DOMINIC JOHN

Liltingly *(con sentimento)*

A Blos-som Fell___ from off a tree,___ It set-tled soft-ly on the lips you turned to me,___ The Gip-sies say, And I know why,___ A fall-ing blos-som on-ly

FOR ALL WE KNOW

Words by SAM M LEWIS
Music by J FRED COOTS

LET THERE BE LOVE

Words by IAN GRANT
Music by LIONEL RAND

REFRAIN

Let there be you_____ And let there be me_____
Let there be you_____ And let there be me_____

Let there be moon - light_____ o - ver the sea_____
Let there be oys - ters_____ un - der the sea_____

Let there be light_____ to en-light-en our day_____ Chas-ing the
Let there be wind_____ and oc-cas-ion-al rain_____ Small cor-ner

sha - dows_____ of dark-ness a - way_____ Let there be
ta - bles_____ and spark-ling cham pagne_____ Let there be

10

MONA LISA

Words and Music by
JAY LIVINGSTON and RAY EVANS

12

13

PRETEND

Words and Music by LEW DOUGLAS,
CLIFF PARMAN and FRANK LAVERE

RAMBLIN' ROSE

Words and Music by
NOEL SHERMAN and JOE SHERMAN

SMILE

Words by JOHN TURNER and GEOFFREY PARSONS
Music by CHARLES CHAPLIN

THOSE LAZY HAZY CRAZY DAYS OF SUMMER

Words by CHARLES TOBIAS
Music by HANS CARSTE

TOO YOUNG

Words by SYLVIA DEE
Music by SID LIPPMAN

23

UNFORGETTABLE

Words and Music
by IRVING GORDON

THE VERY THOUGHT OF YOU

Words and Music
by RAY NOBLE

VERSE

1. I don't need your pho-to-graph,___ To keep__ by my bed; Your pic-ture is
2. I hold you re-spon-si-ble,___ I'll take__ it to law, I ne-ver have

Ab   Bb7   Eb11   Eb7   Abmaj7   Ab   Bdim

al-ways in__ my head.___ I don't need your por-trait, dear,___
felt like this__ be-fore.___ I'm su-ing for da-ma-ges___

Bbm7   Cm   Ab   Eb7   Ab   Bb13

__ To call you to mind,___ For sleep-ing or wak-ing, dear,__ I find___
__ Ex-cu-ses won't do,___ I'll on-ly be sat-is-fied__ with you.___

Eb7   Edim Fm   Abm6 Bb11 Bb13   Bbm7   Eb7

REFRAIN

WHEN I FALL IN LOVE

Words by EDWARD HEYMAN
Music by VICTOR YOUNG

When I fall in love it will be for - ev-er, Or I'll nev-er fall in

love._____ In a rest - less world like this is, love is end-ed be-fore it's be-

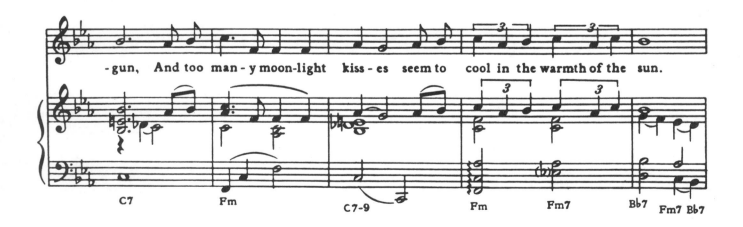

-gun, And too man - y moon-light kiss - es seem to cool in the warmth of the sun.

SOMEWHERE ALONG THE WAY

Words by SAMMY GALLOP
Music by KURT ADAMS

REFRAIN Slowly

Printed in England
Panda Press · Haverhill · Suffolk • 11/92